Trace the dotted lines. Practise using your pencil.

Add a grape to each group.

Draw raindrops coming from the clouds.

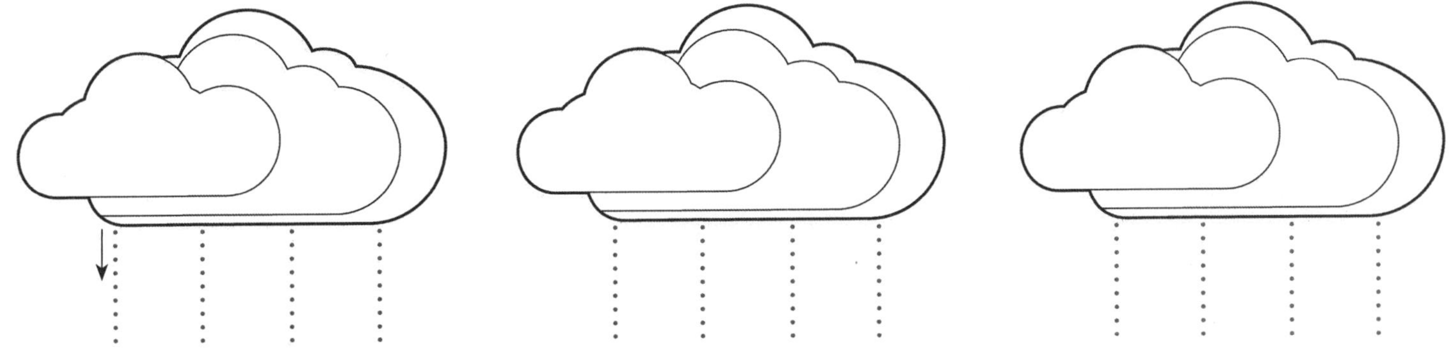

Add a row to the rainbows.

Add a smile to the crabs' faces.

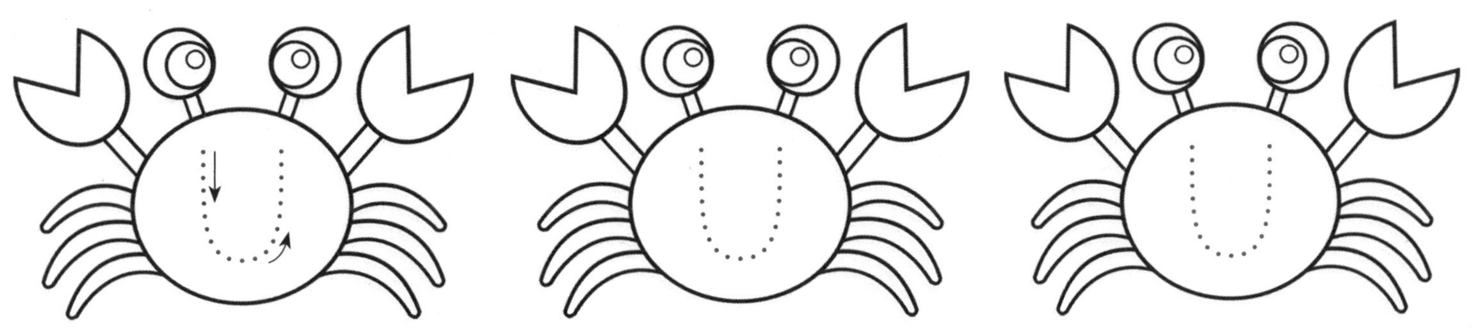

Trace the dotted lines. Practise using your pencil.

Add lines to the buses.

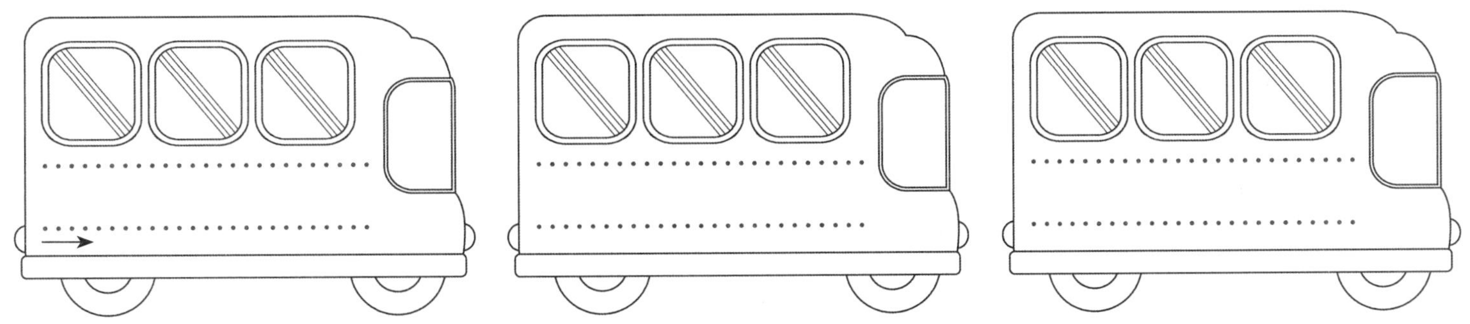

Add a stem to the flowers.

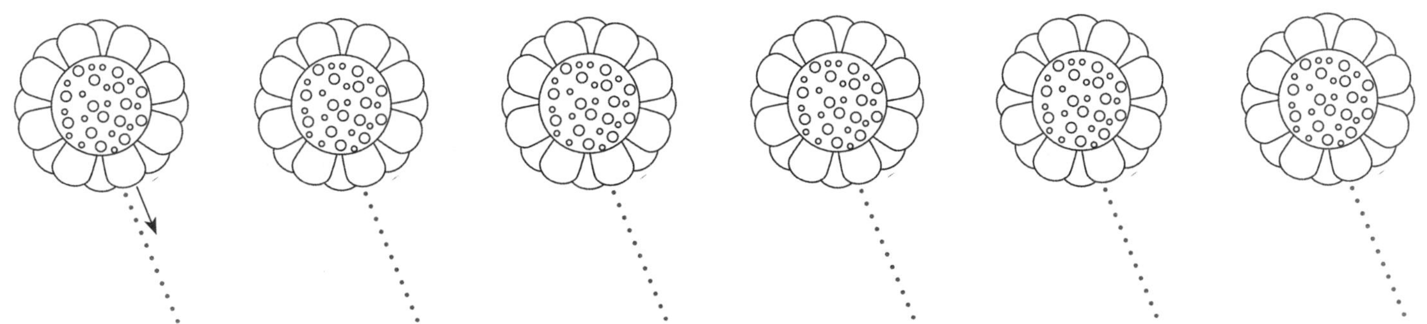

Add a side to the kites.

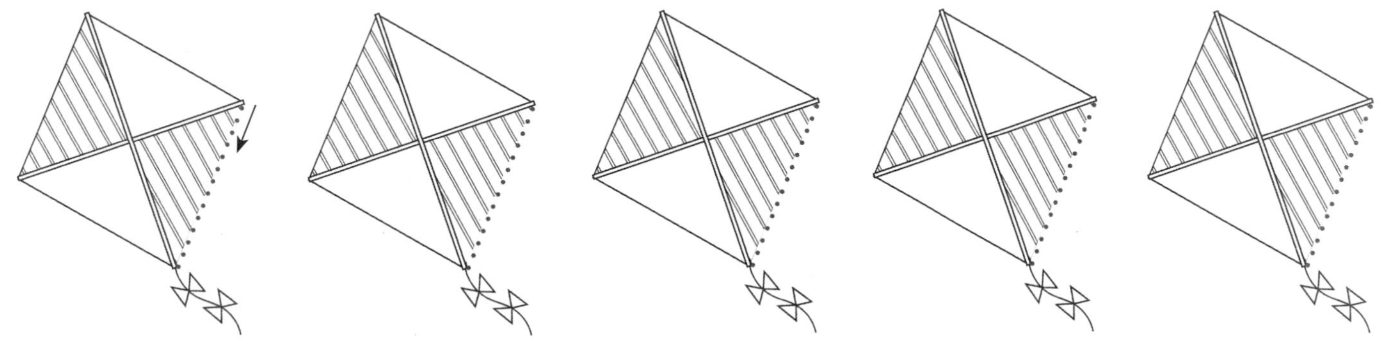

Add a pattern to the drums.

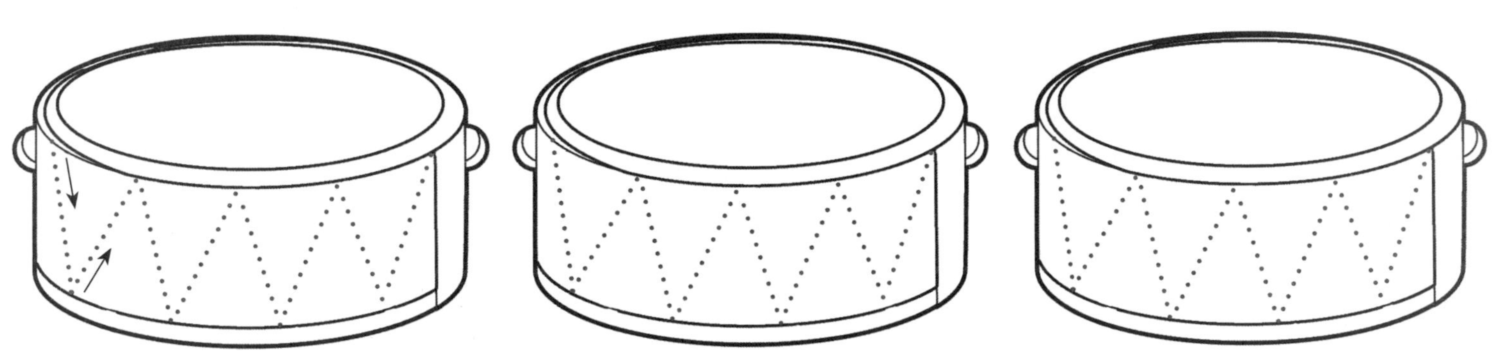

Colour the letters.

Aa

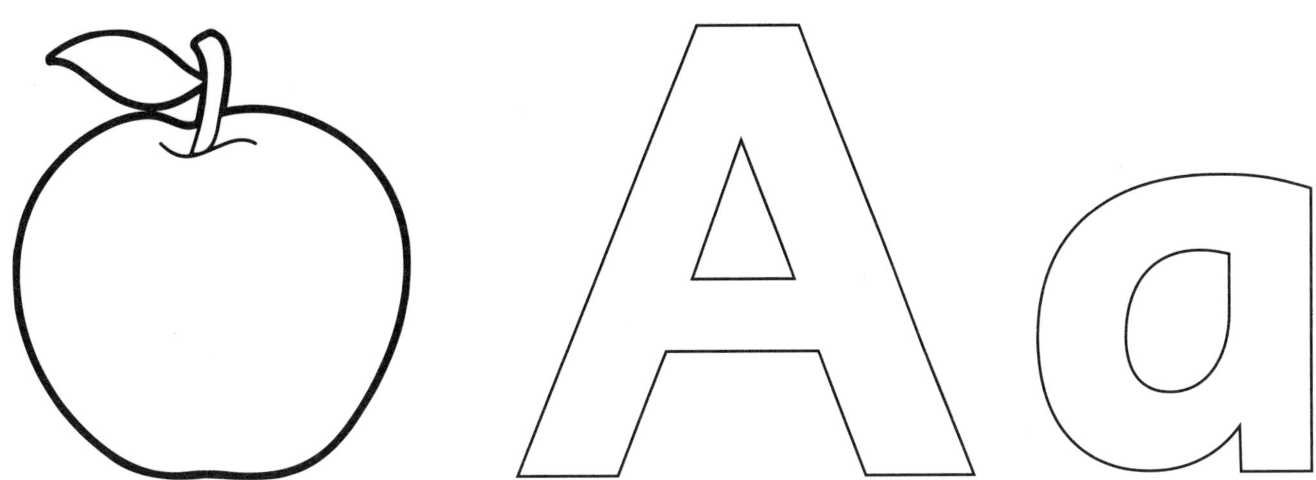

Now practise tracing the letters.

A A A A A A A

A A A A A A A

a a a a a a a

a a a a a a a

Colour the letters.

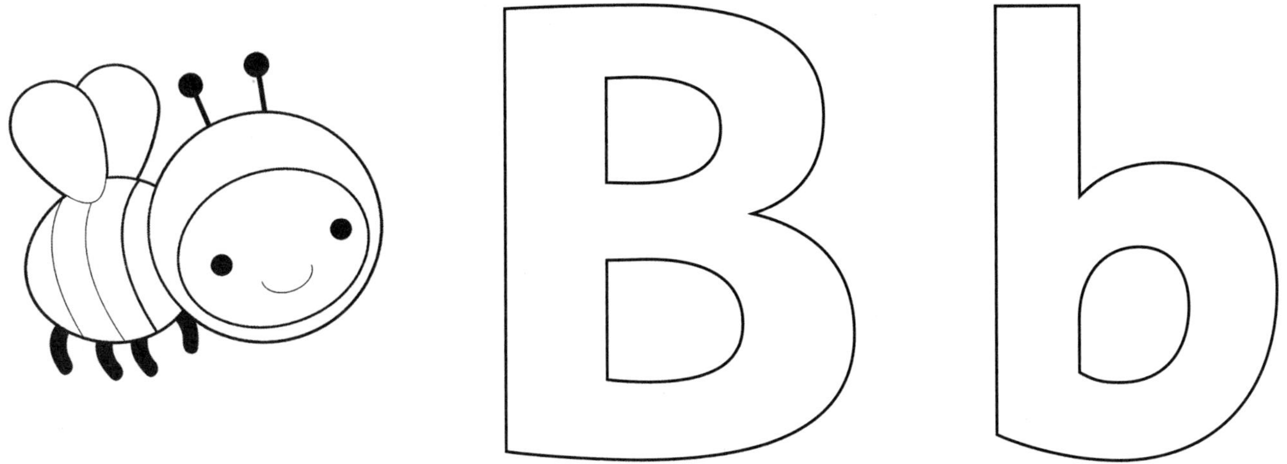

Now practise tracing the letters.

Colour the letters.

Cc

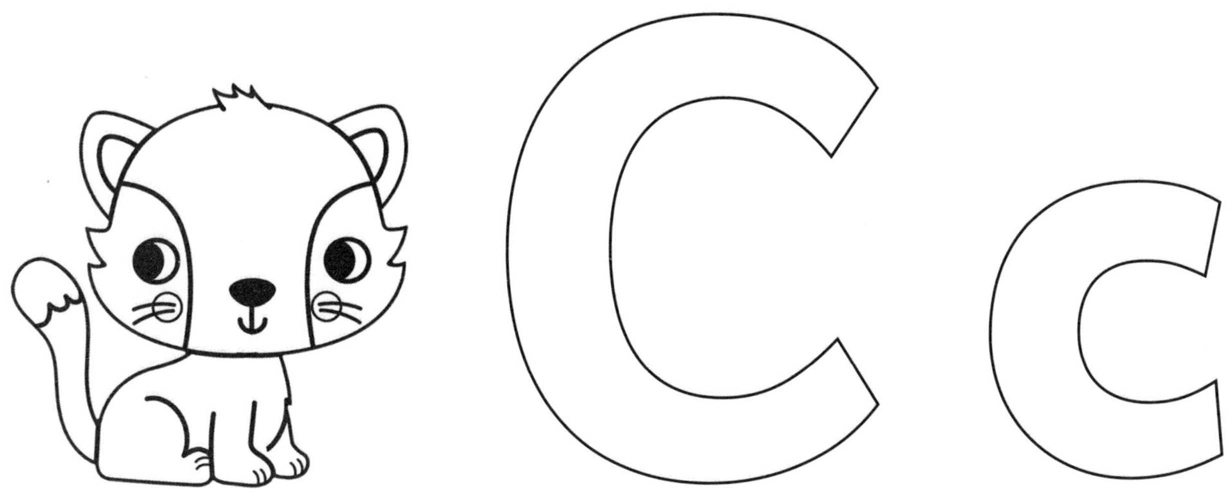

Now practise tracing the letters.

C C C C C C C

C C C C C C C

c c c c c c c

c c c c c c c

Colour the letters.

Dd

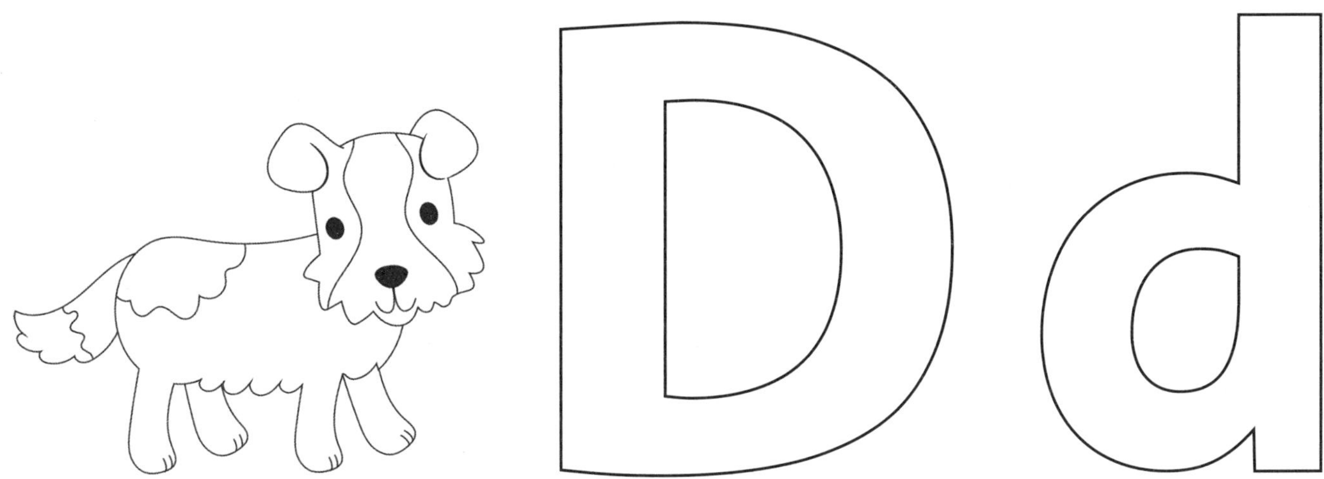

Now practise tracing the letters.

D D D D D D D

D D D D D D D

d d d d d d d

d d d d d d d

Colour the letters.

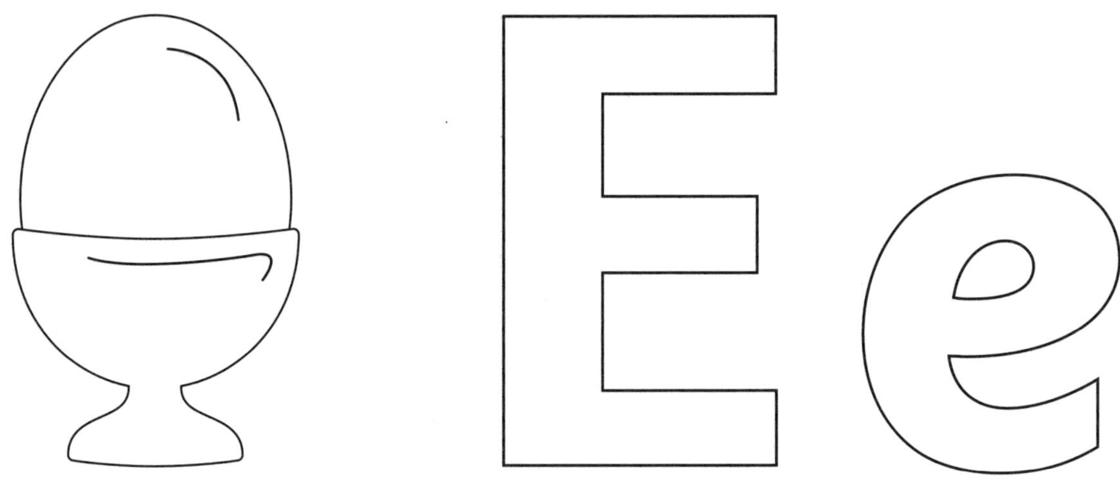

Now practise tracing the letters.

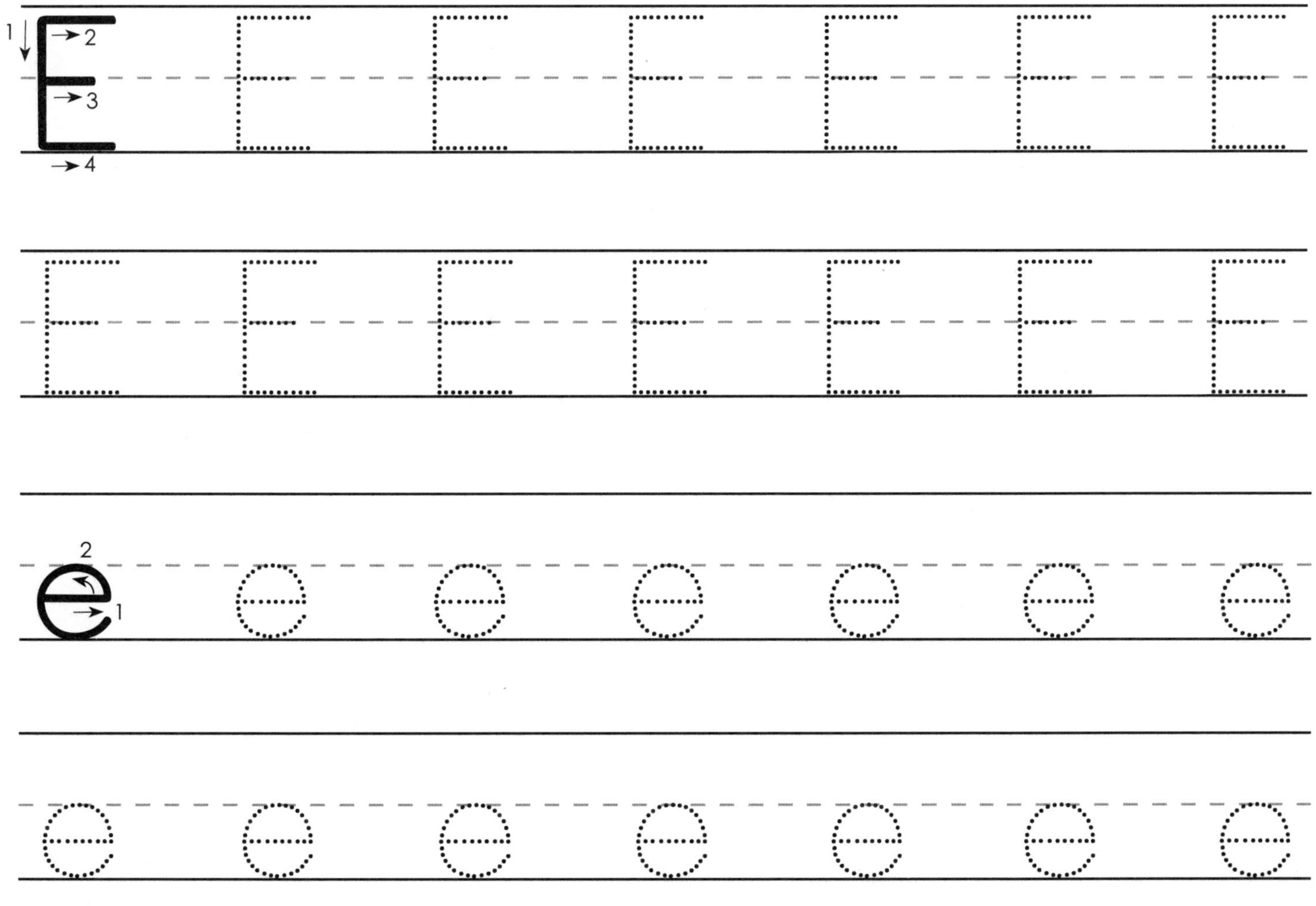

E E E E E E E

E E E E E E E

e e e e e e e

e e e e e e e

Colour the letters.

F f

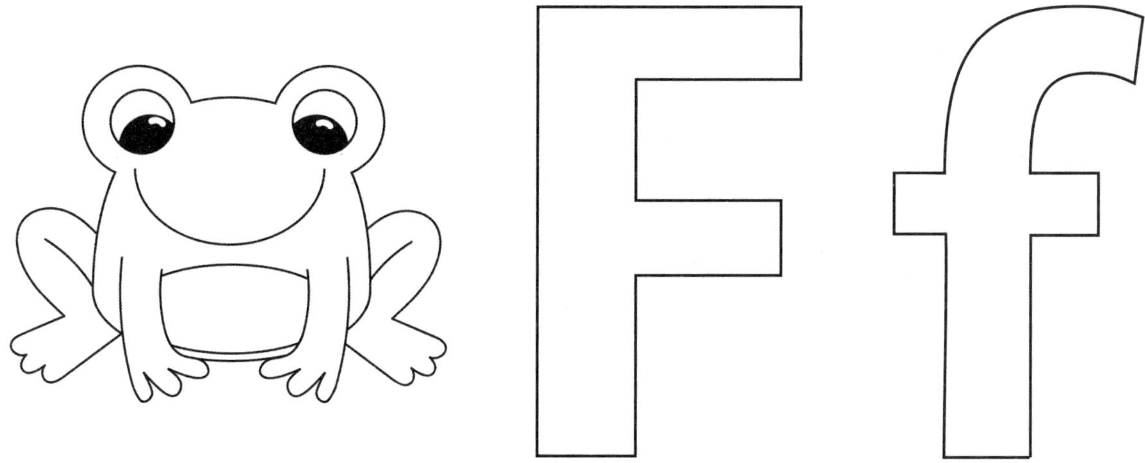

Now practise tracing the letters.

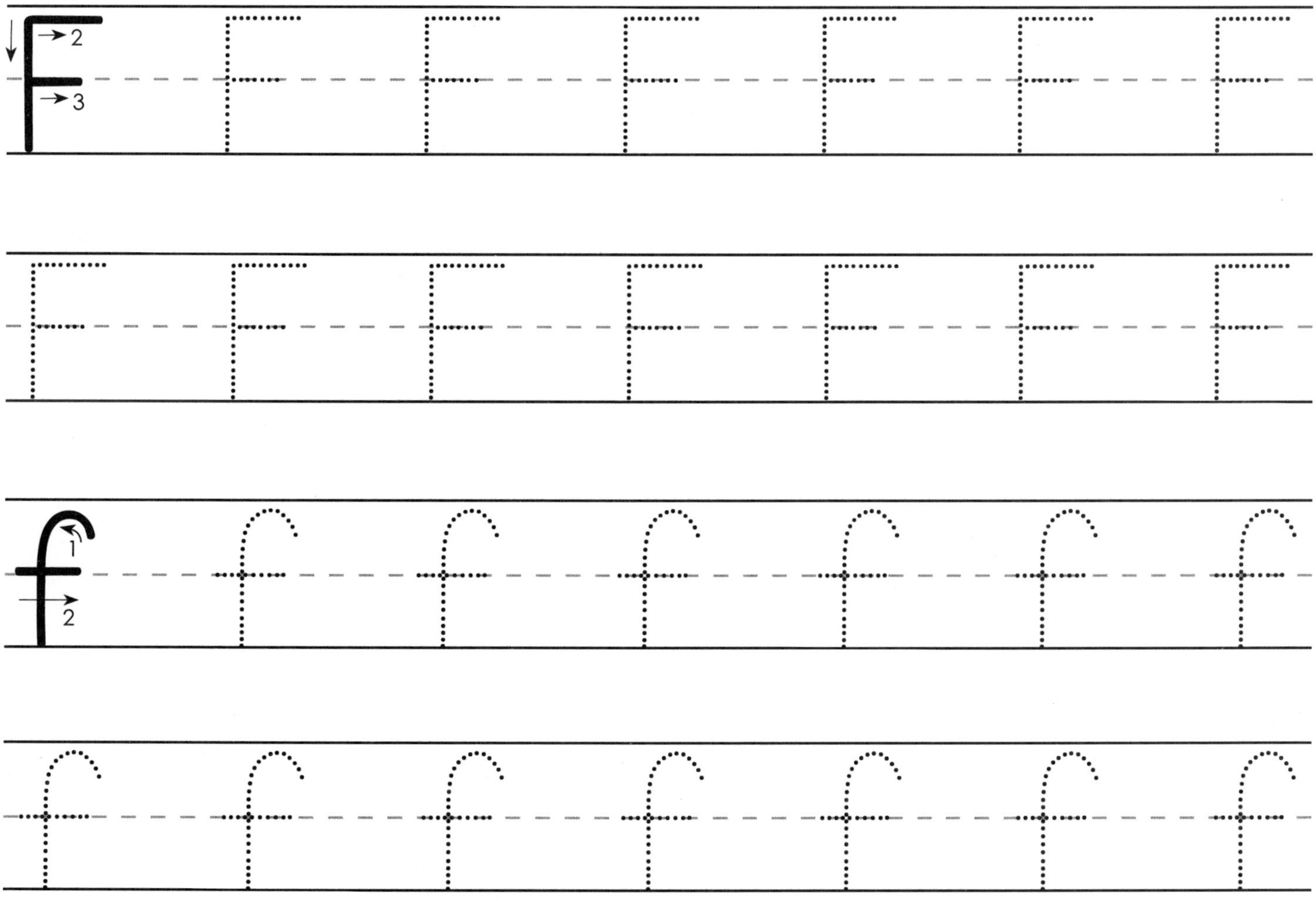

Colour the letters.

G g

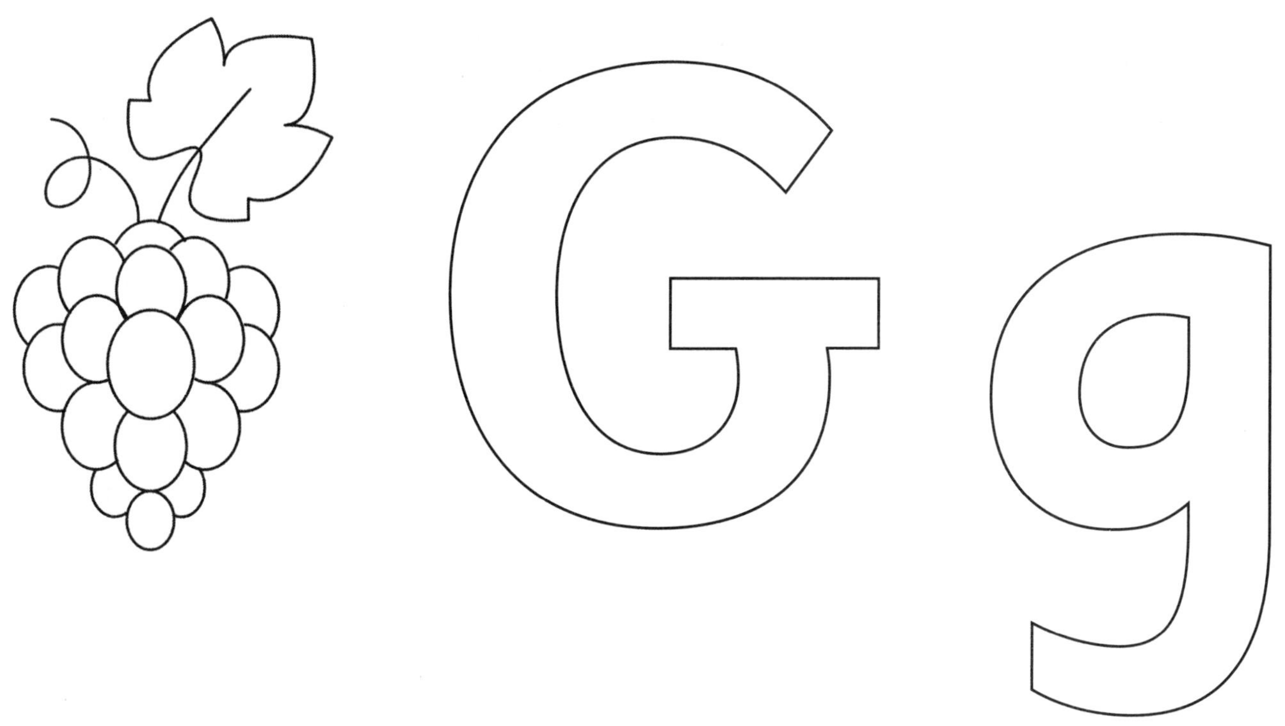

Now practise tracing the letters.

Colour the letters.

H h

Now practise tracing the letters.

H H H H H H H

H H H H H H H

h h h h h h h

h h h h h h h

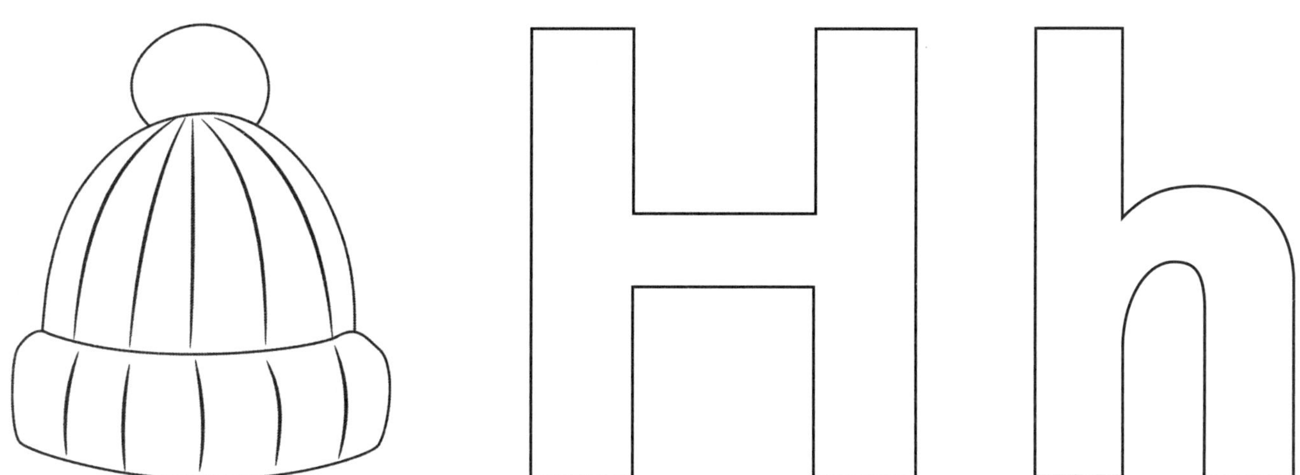

Colour the letters.

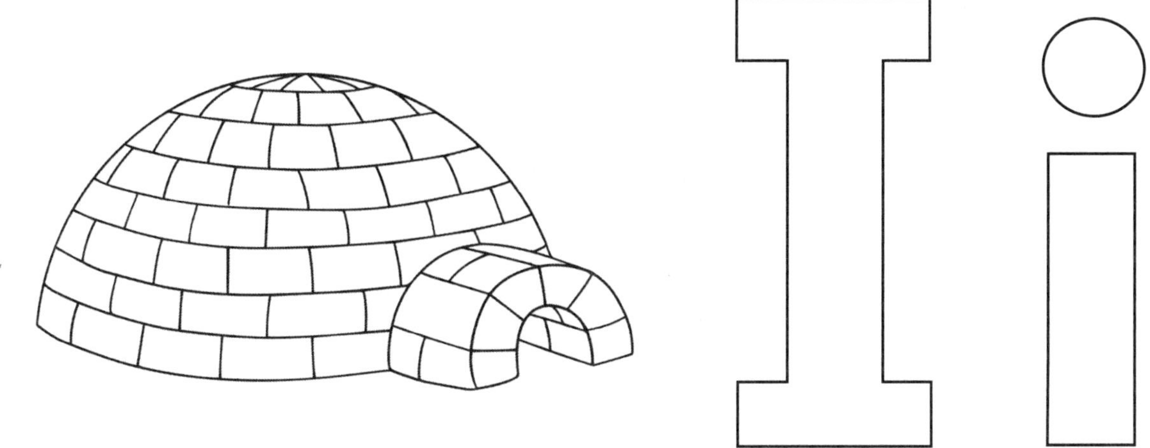

Now practise tracing the letters.

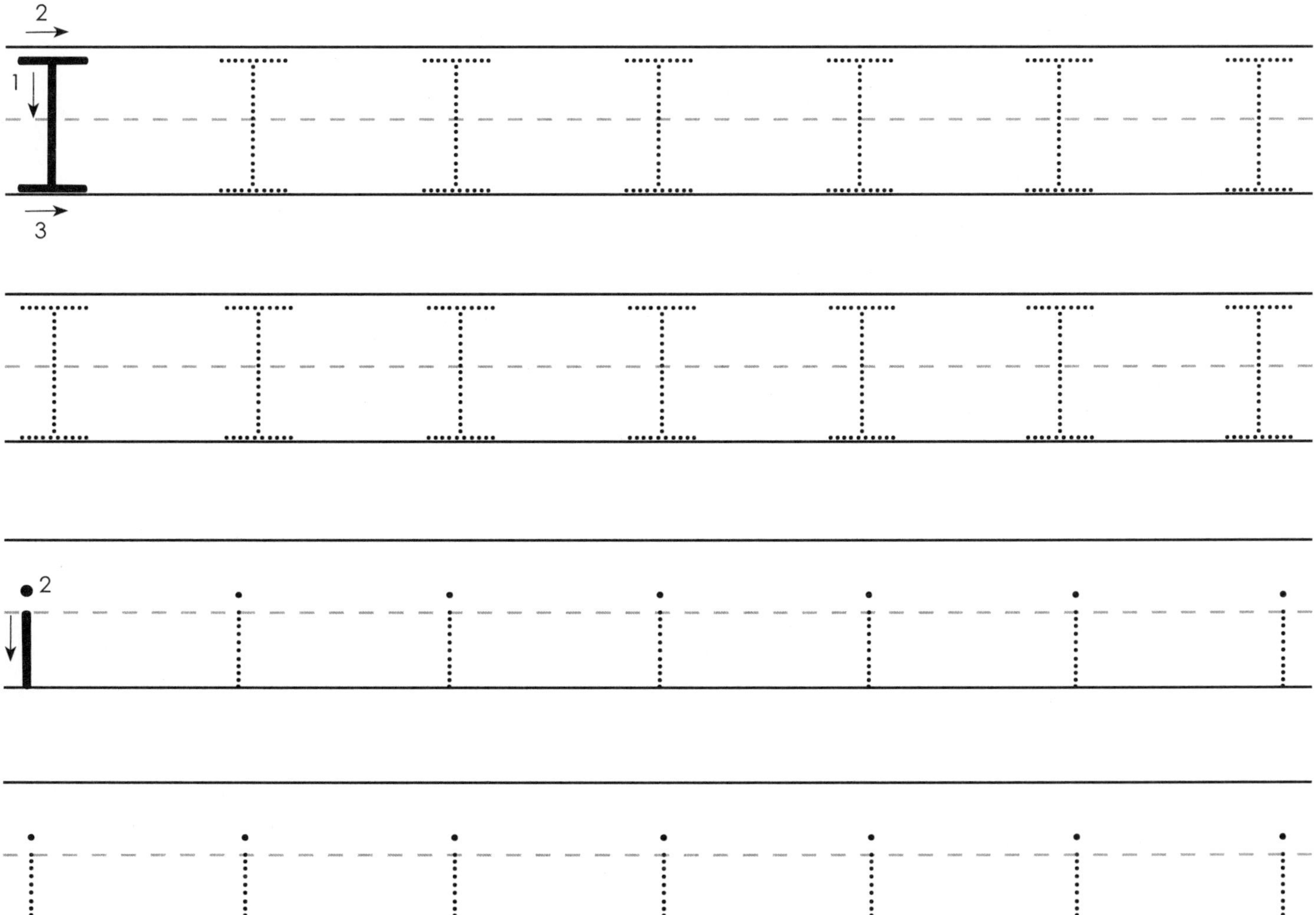

I I I I I I I

I I I I I I I

i i i i i i i

i i i i i i i

Colour the letters.

J j

Now practise tracing the letters.

J J J J J J J

J J J J J J J

j j j j j j j

j j j j j j j

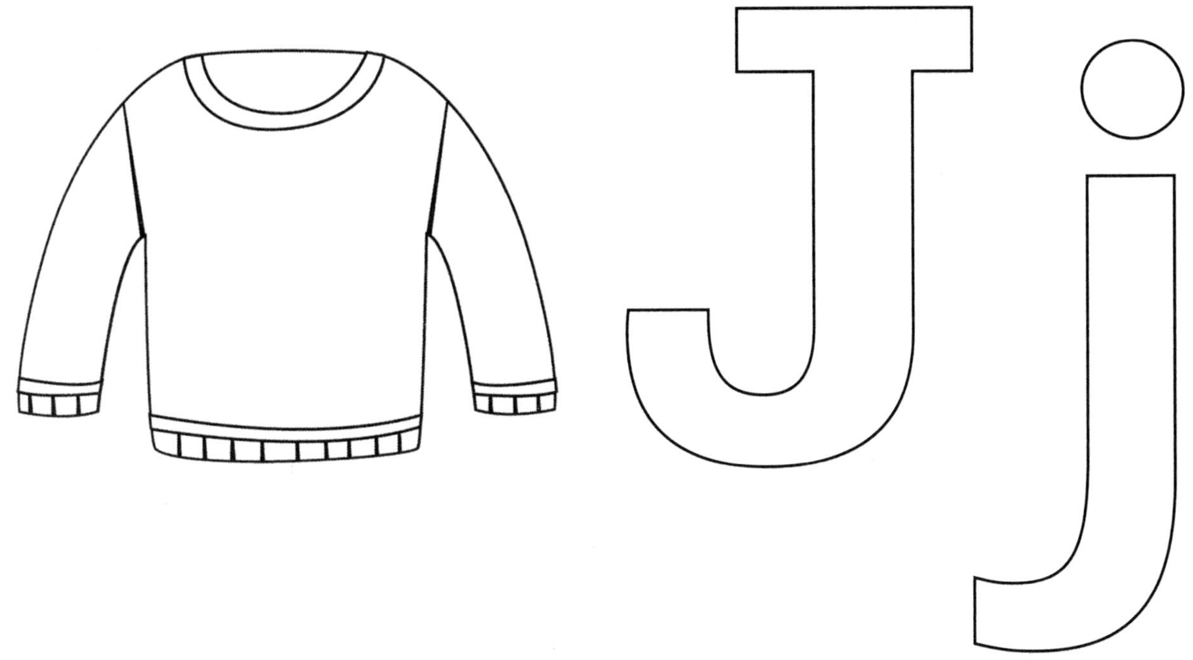

Colour the letters.

Now practise tracing the letters.

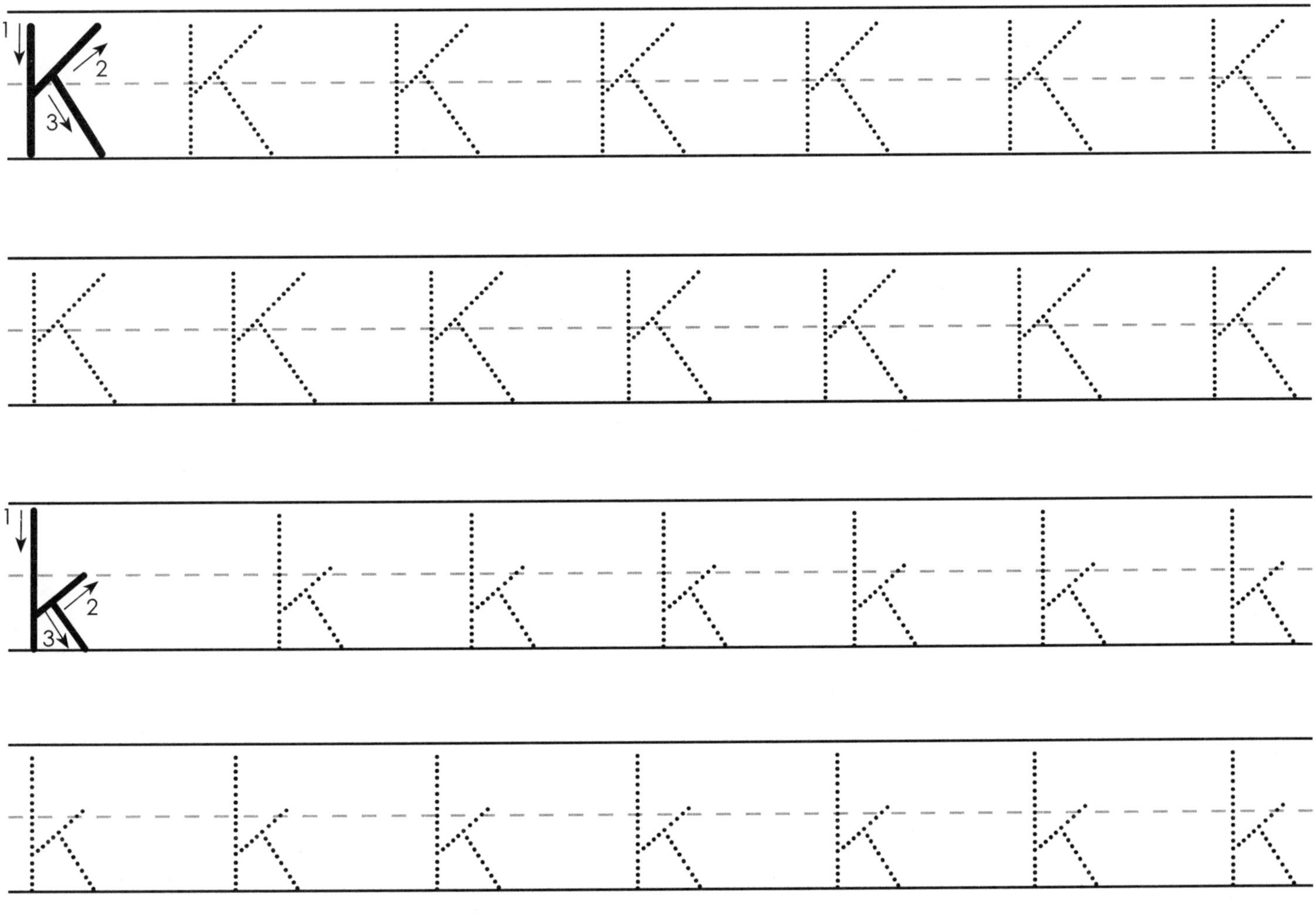

K K K K K K K

K K K K K K K

k k k k k k k

k k k k k k k

Colour the letters.

Now practise tracing the letters.

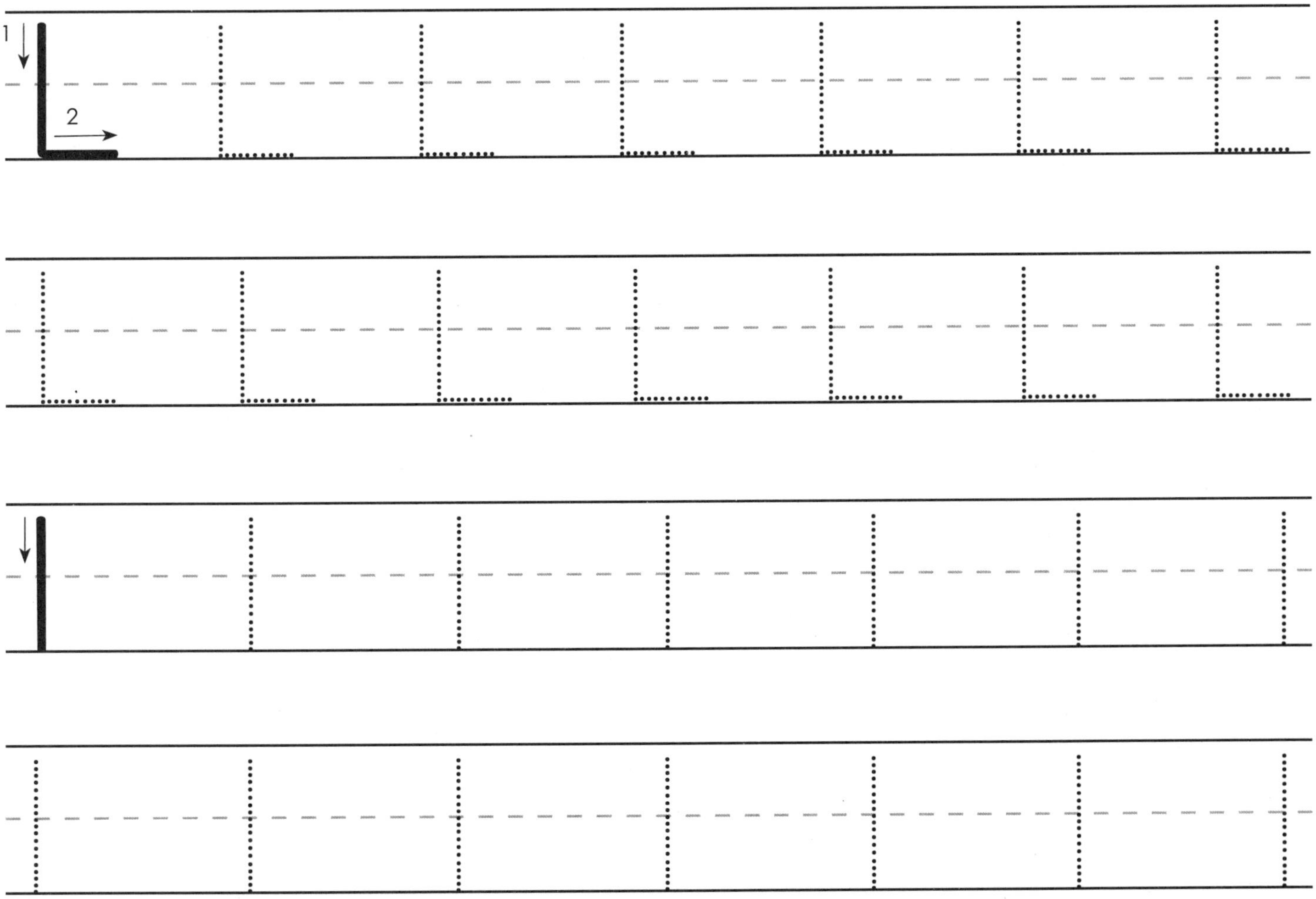

1 2

Colour the letters.

Mm

Now practise tracing the letters.

M M M M M M M

M M M M M M M

m m m m m m m

m m m m m m m

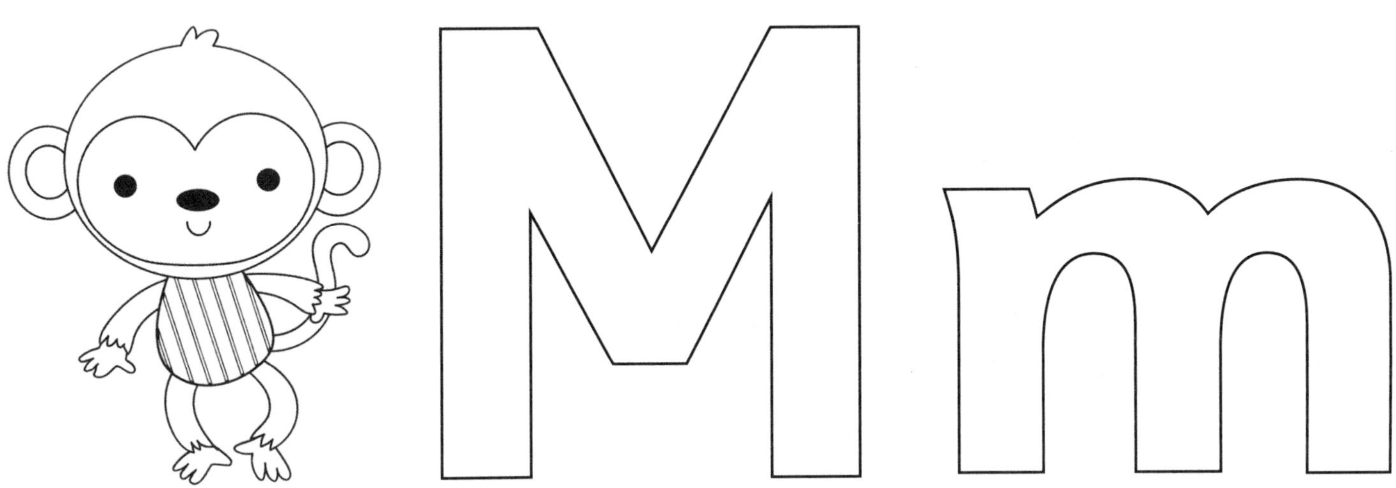

Colour the letters.

Nn

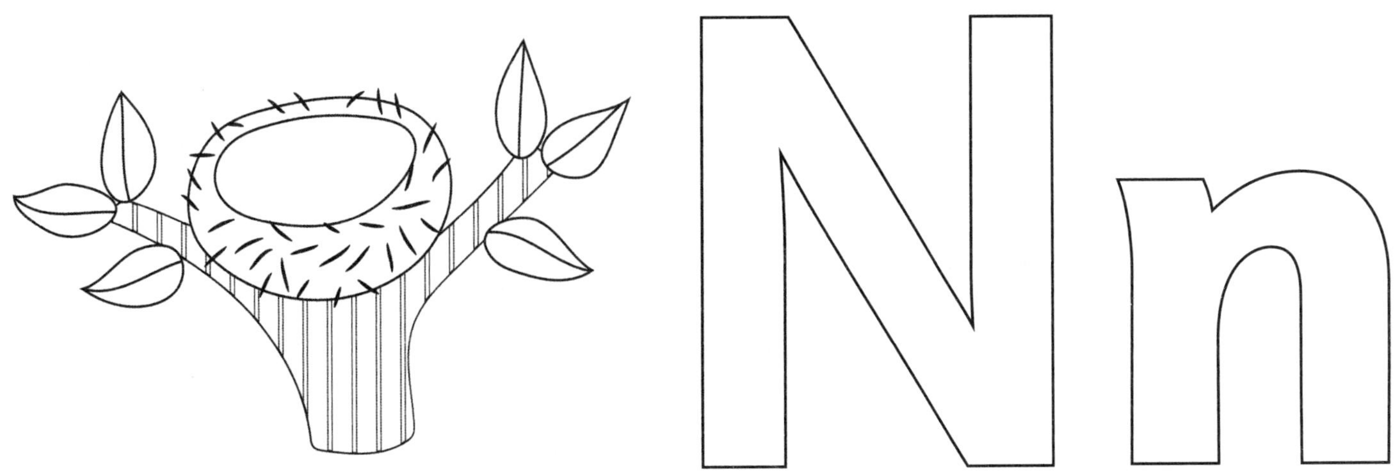

Now practise tracing the letters.

N N N N N N N

N N N N N N N

n n n n n n n

n n n n n n n

Colour the letters.

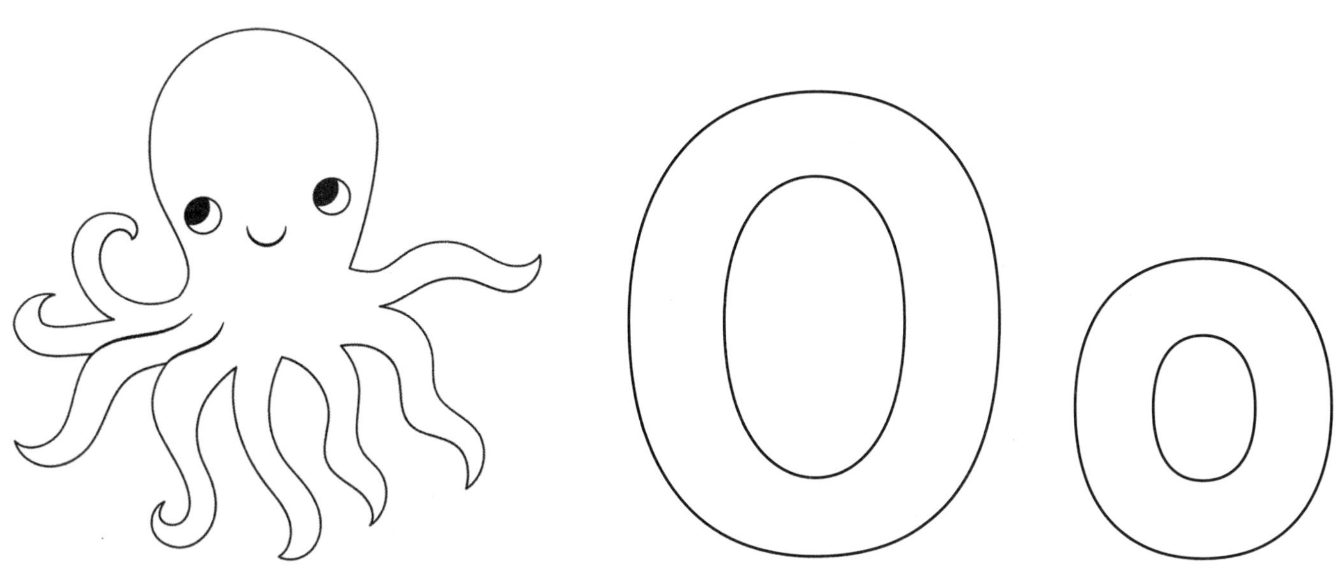

Now practise tracing the letters.

Colour the letters.

Now practise tracing the letters.

P P P P P P P

P P P P P P P

p p p p p p p

p p p p p p p

Colour the letters.

Now practise tracing the letters.

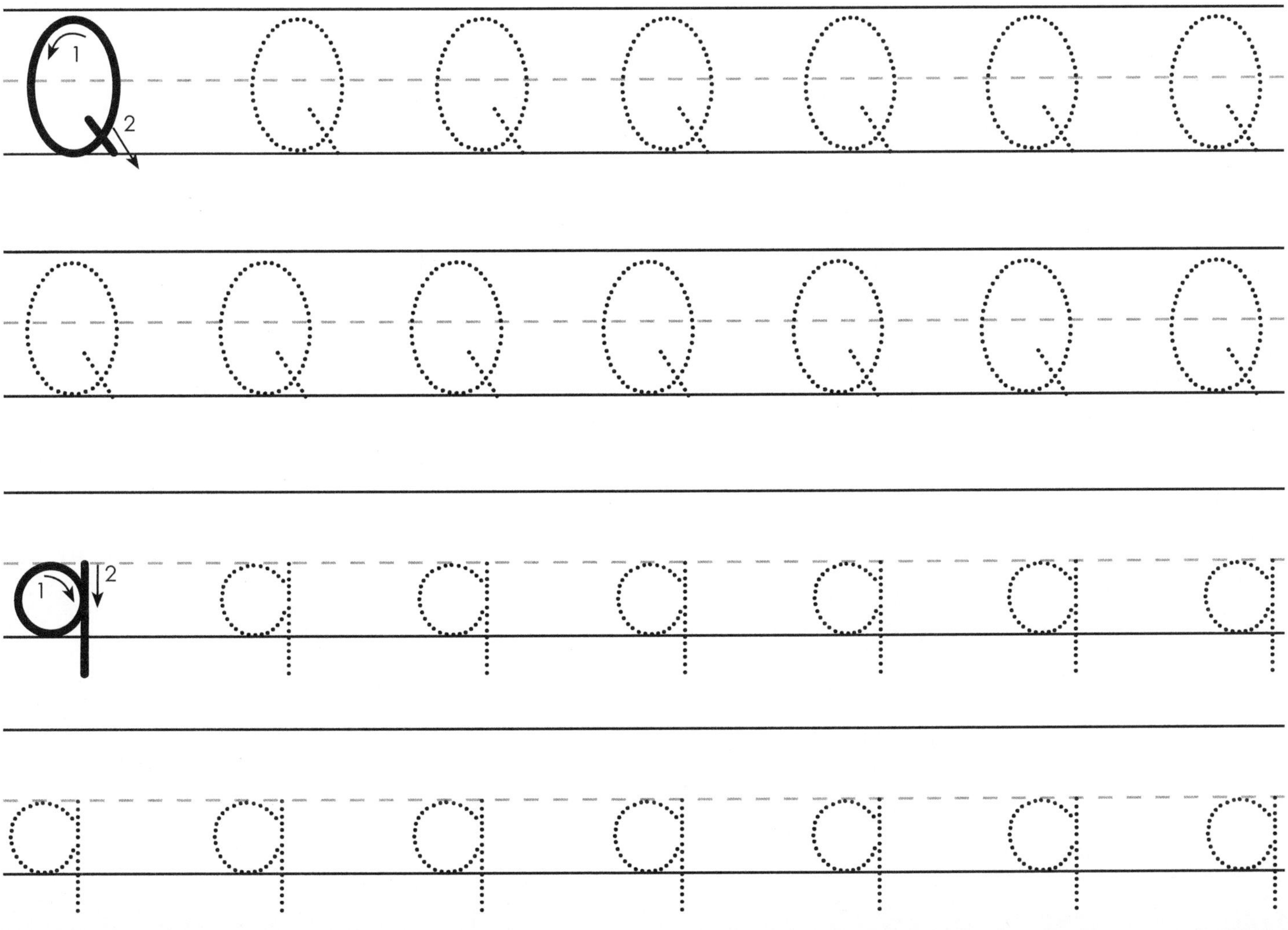

Q Q Q Q Q Q Q

Q Q Q Q Q Q Q

q q q q q q q

q q q q q q q

Colour the letters.

Rr

Now practise tracing the letters.

R R R R R R R

R R R R R R R

r r r r r r r

r r r r r r r

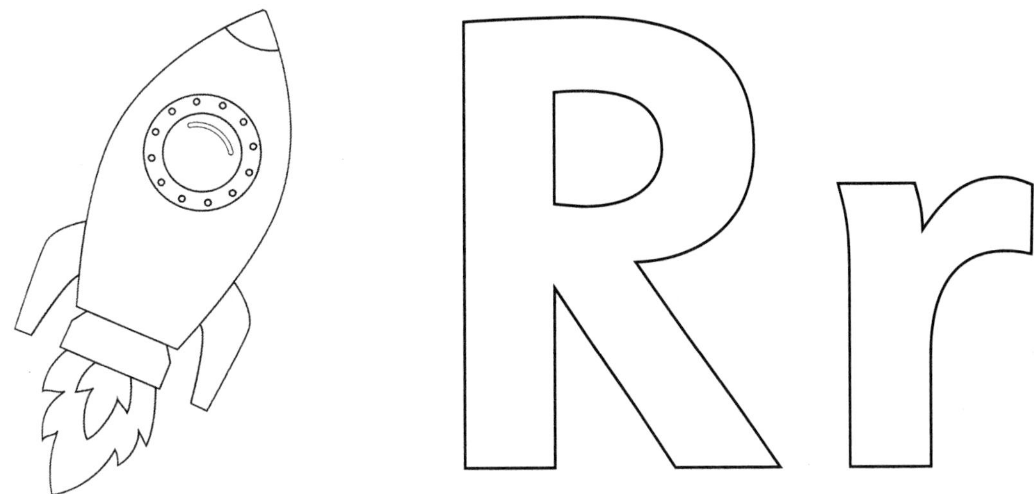

Colour the letters.

Ss

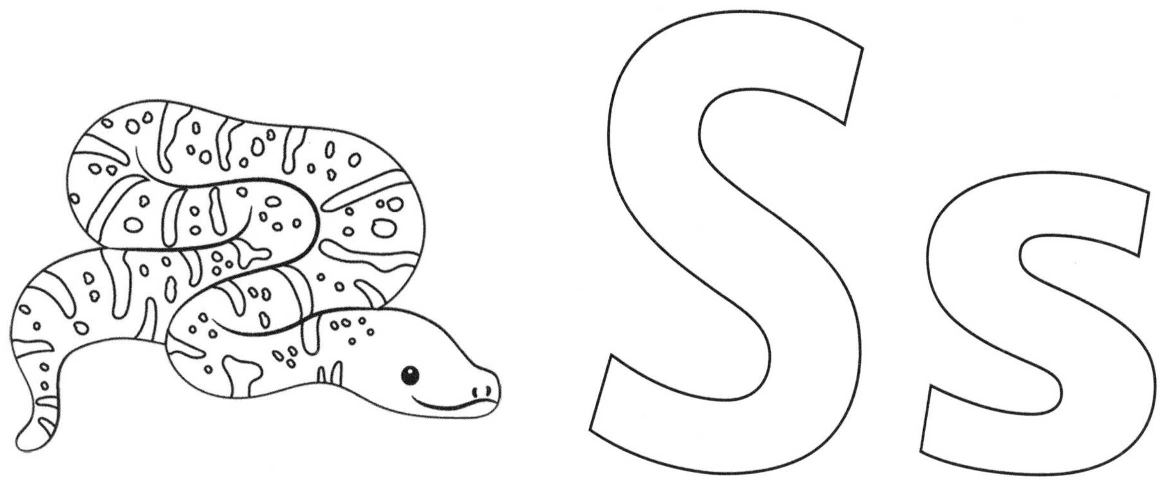

Now practise tracing the letters.

S S S S S S S

S S S S S S S

s s s s s s s

s s s s s s s

Colour the letters.

Now practise tracing the letters.

Colour the letters.

Uu

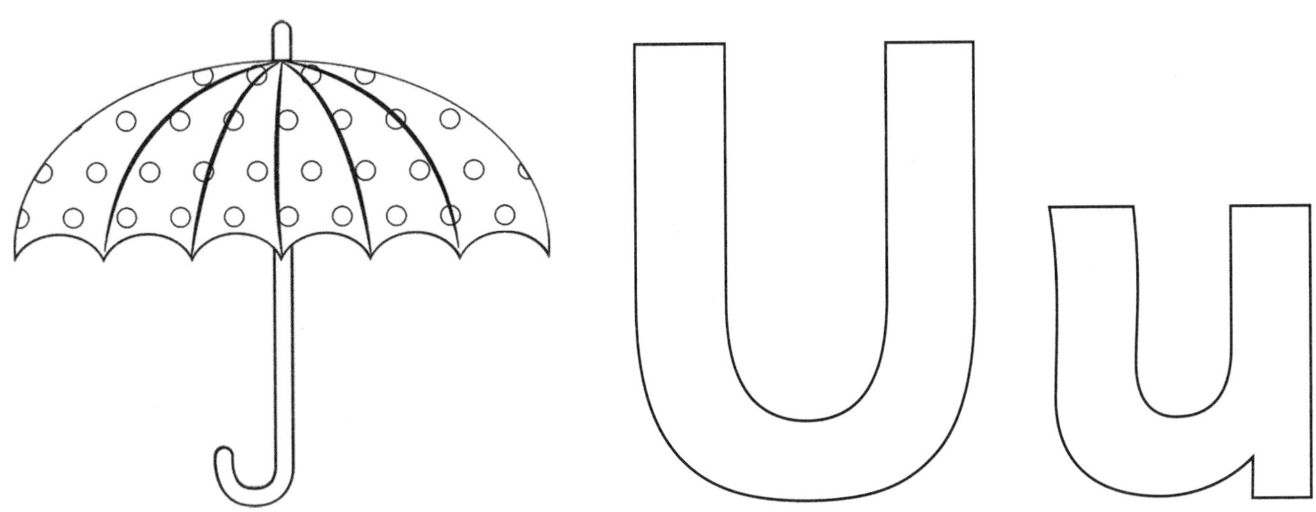

Now practise tracing the letters.

Colour the letters.

V v

Now practise tracing the letters.

V V V V V V V

V V V V V V V

v v v v v v v

v v v v v v v

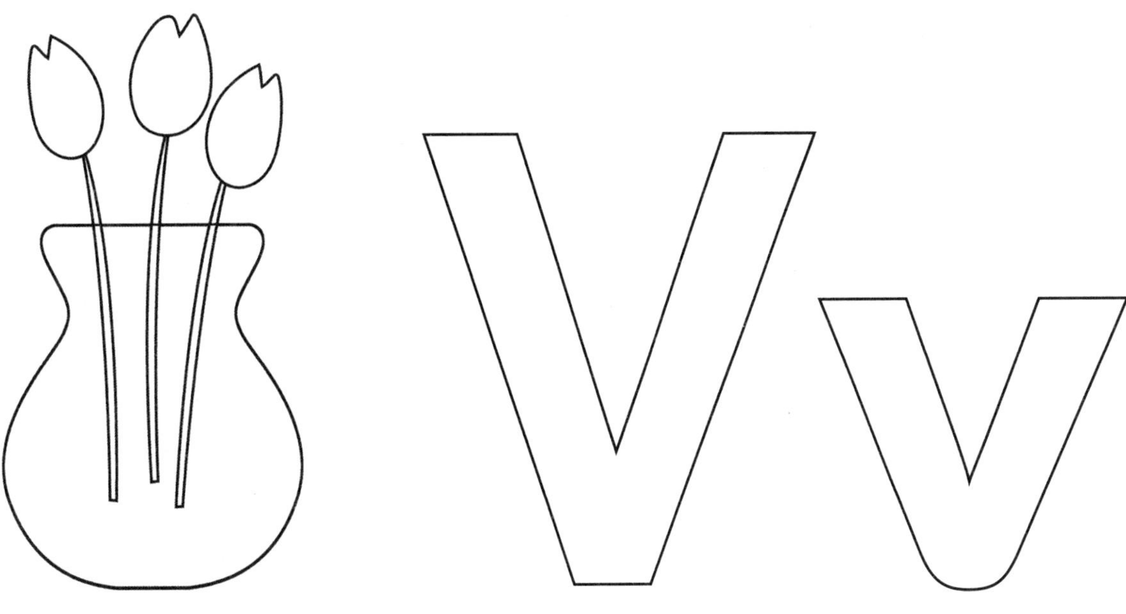

Colour the letters.

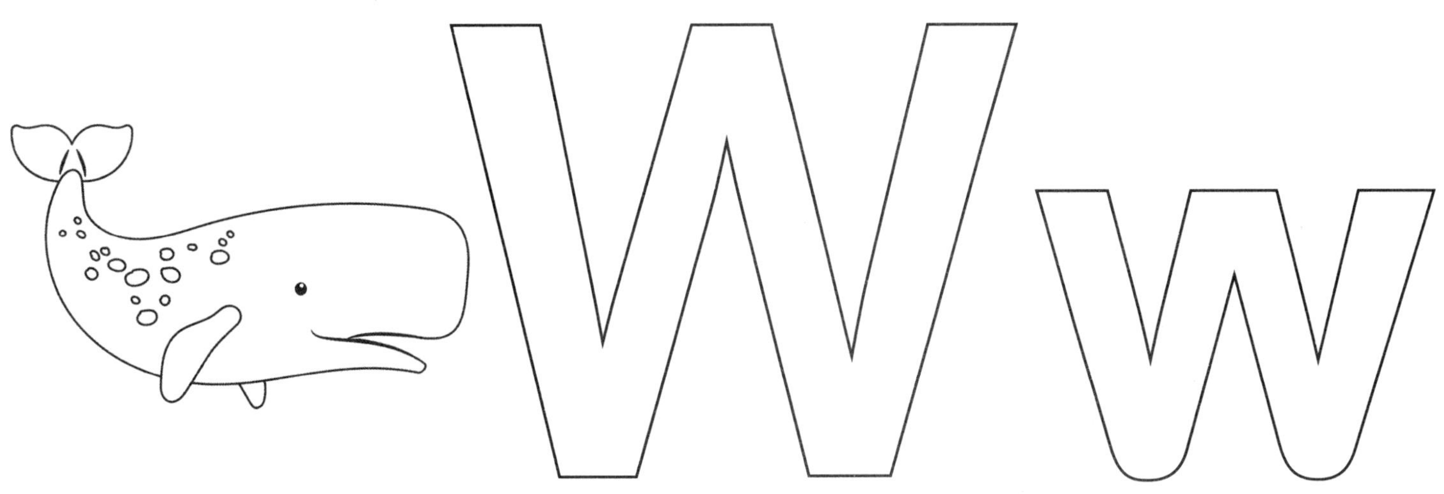

Now practise tracing the letters.

Colour the letters.

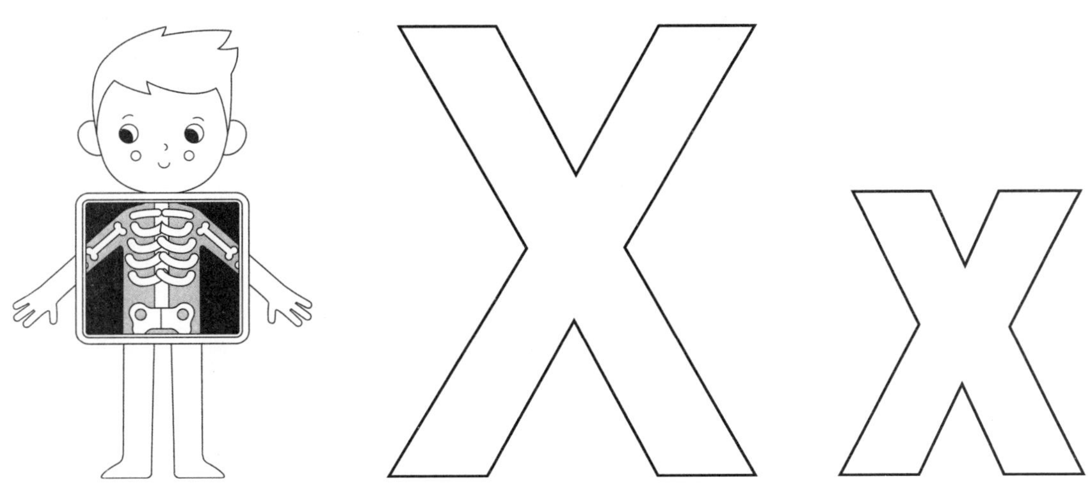

Now practise tracing the letters.

Colour the letters.

Now practise tracing the letters.

Y Y Y Y Y Y Y

Y Y Y Y Y Y Y

y y y y y y y

y y y y y y y

Colour the letters.

Now practise tracing the letters.

Z Z Z Z Z Z Z

Z Z Z Z Z Z Z

z z z z z z z

z z z z z z z

Trace the letters of the alphabet.

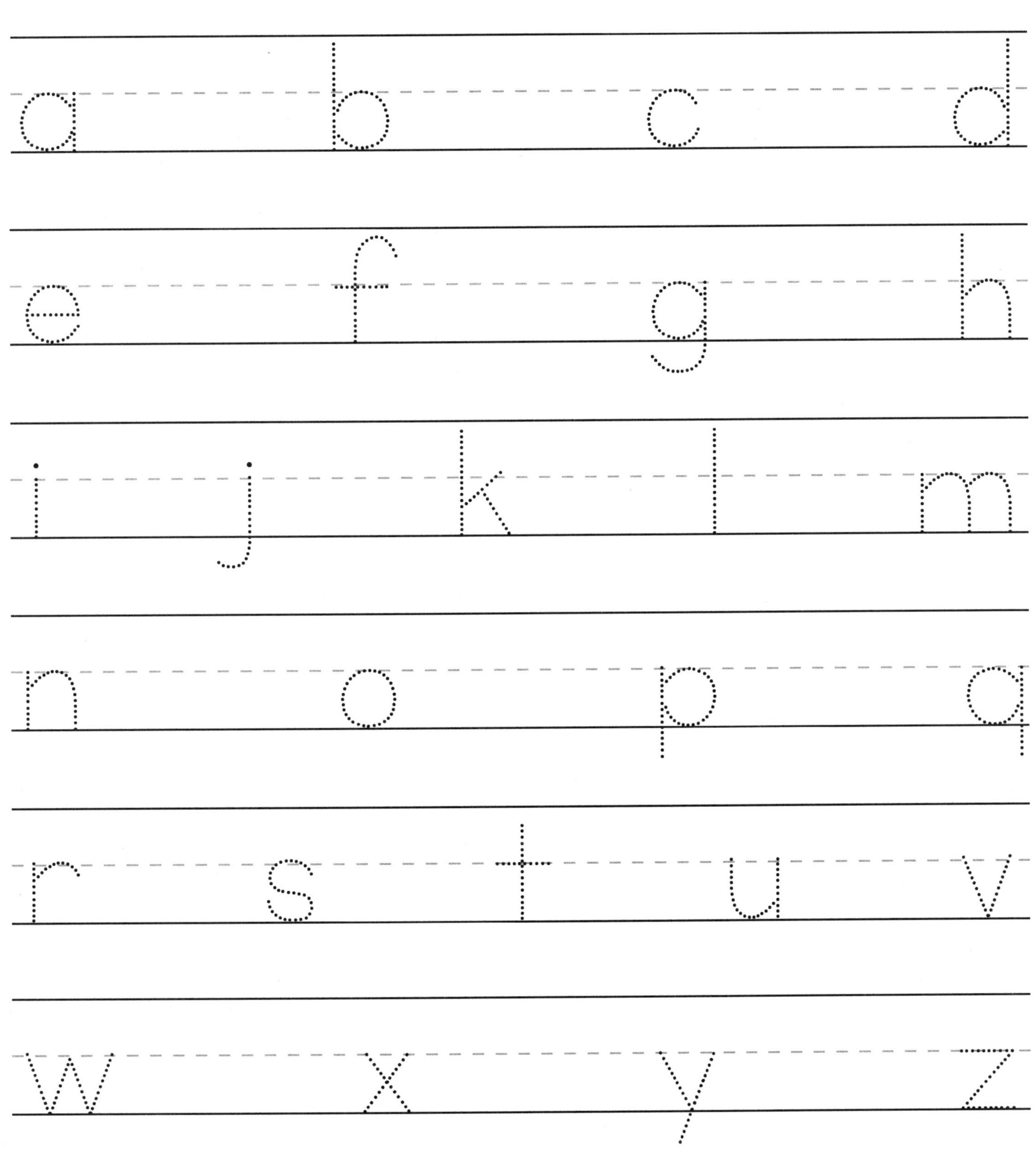

Trace the letters of the alphabet.

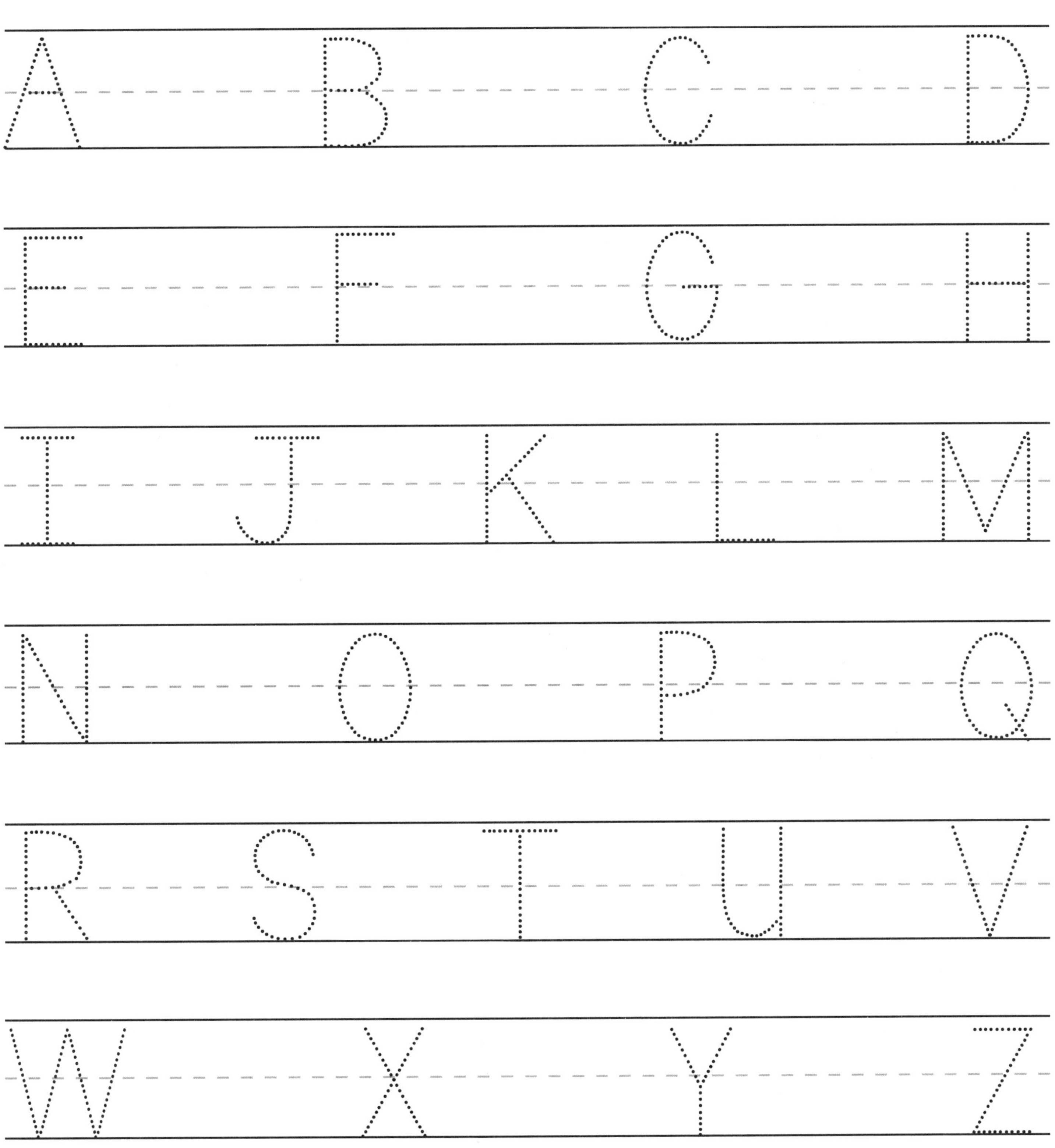

Colour and trace the words.

apple

apple

bee

bee

cat

cat

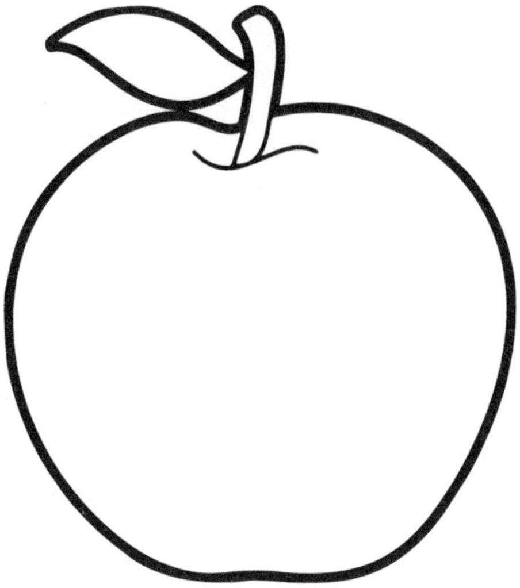

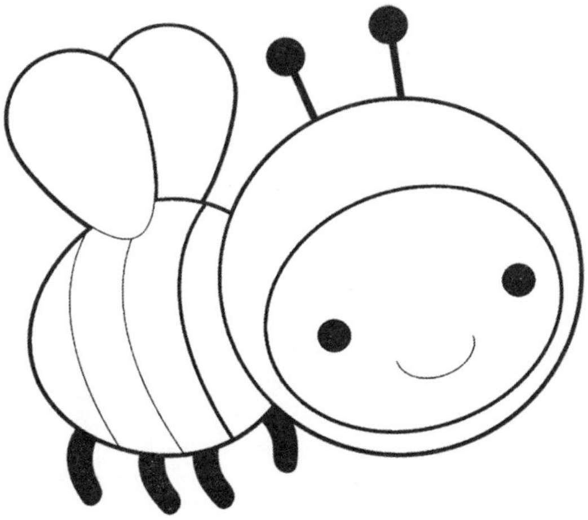

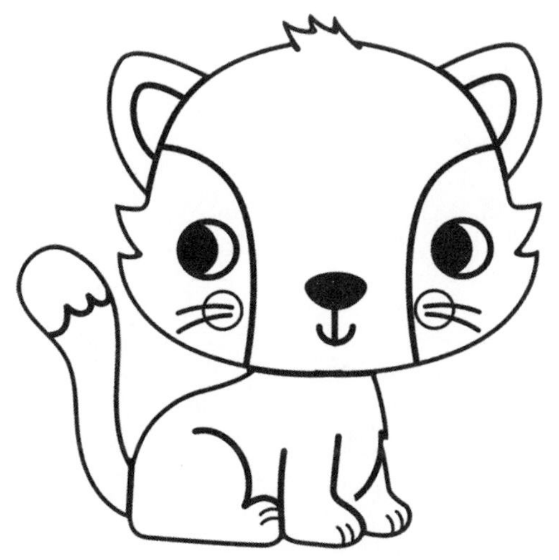

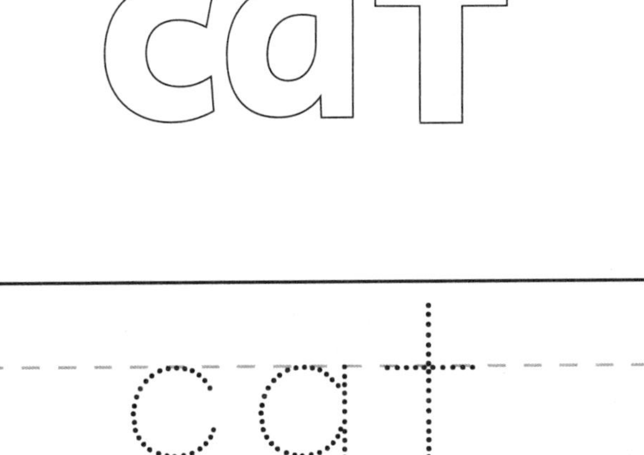

Colour and trace the words.

Colour and trace the words.

grapes

grapes

hat

hat

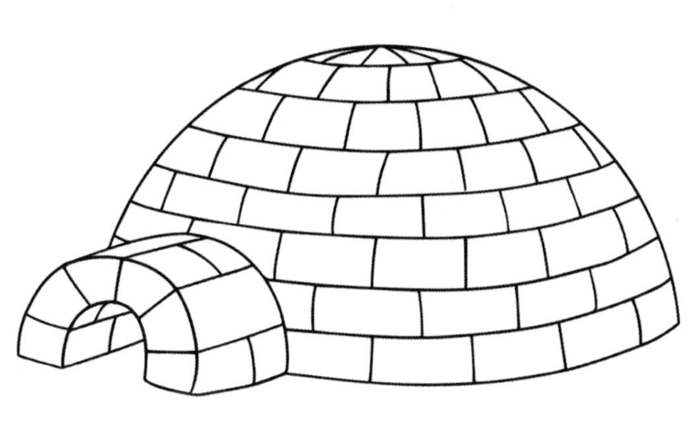

igloo

igloo

Colour and trace the words.

Colour and trace the words.

monkey

monkey

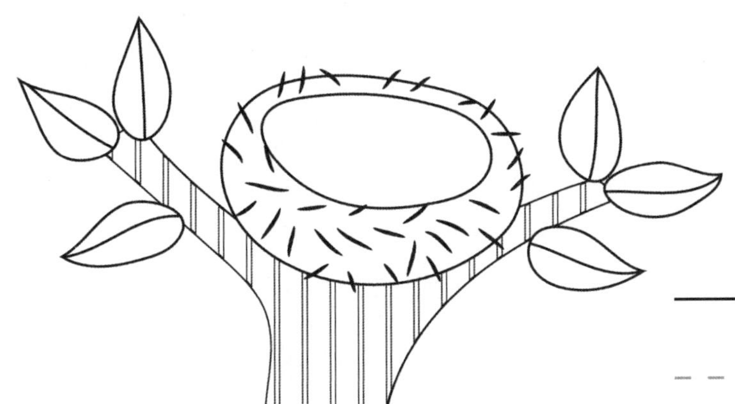

nest

nest

octopus

octopus

Colour and trace the words.

pig

pig

queen

queen

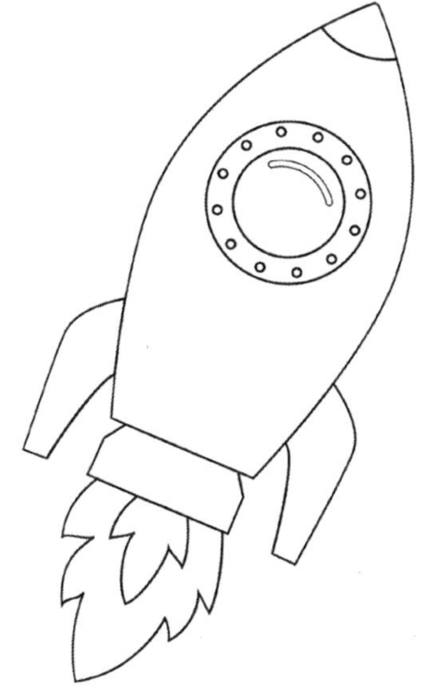

rocket

rocket

Colour and trace the words.

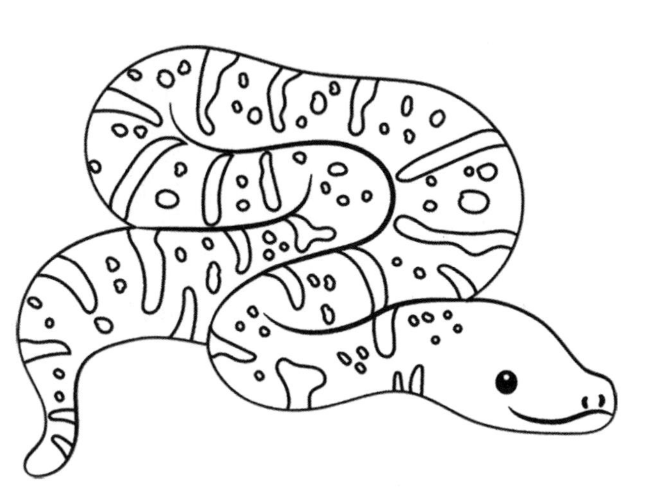

snake

snake

tiger

tiger

umbrella

umbrella

Colour and trace the words.

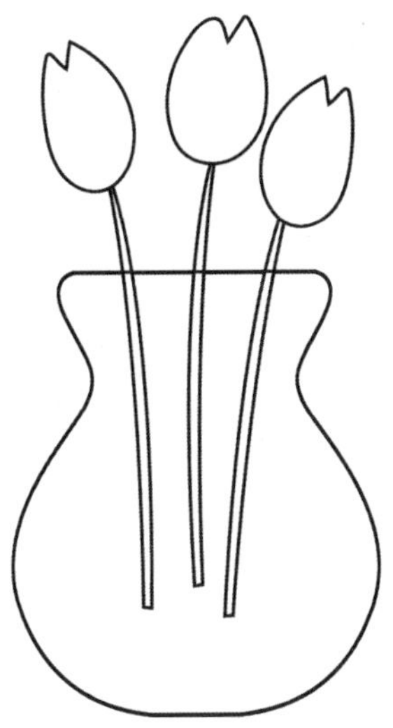

vase

vase

whale

whale

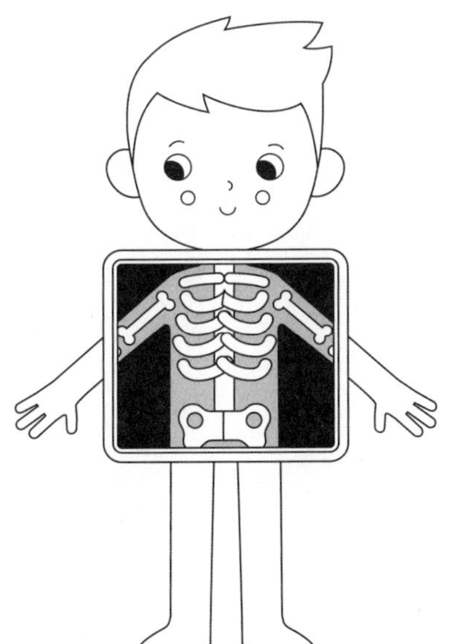

x-ray

x-ray

Colour and trace the words.

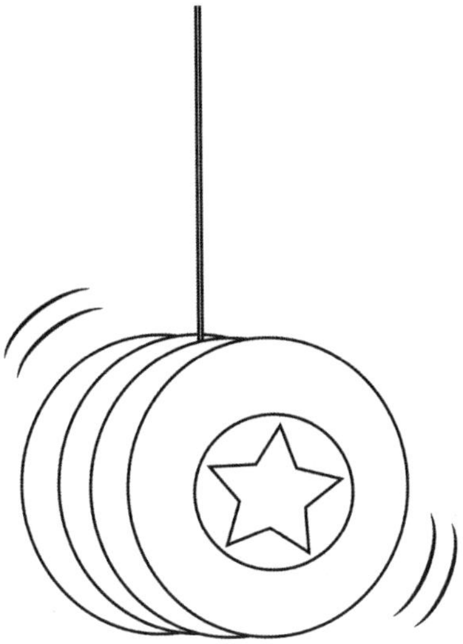

yo-yo

yo-yo

zebra

zebra

Trace the bee paths to the flowers.

Colour and trace the days of the week.

Monday Tuesday

Monday Tuesday

Wednesday

Wednesday

Thursday Friday

Thursday Friday

Saturday Sunday

Saturday Sunday

Colour and trace the words and numbers.

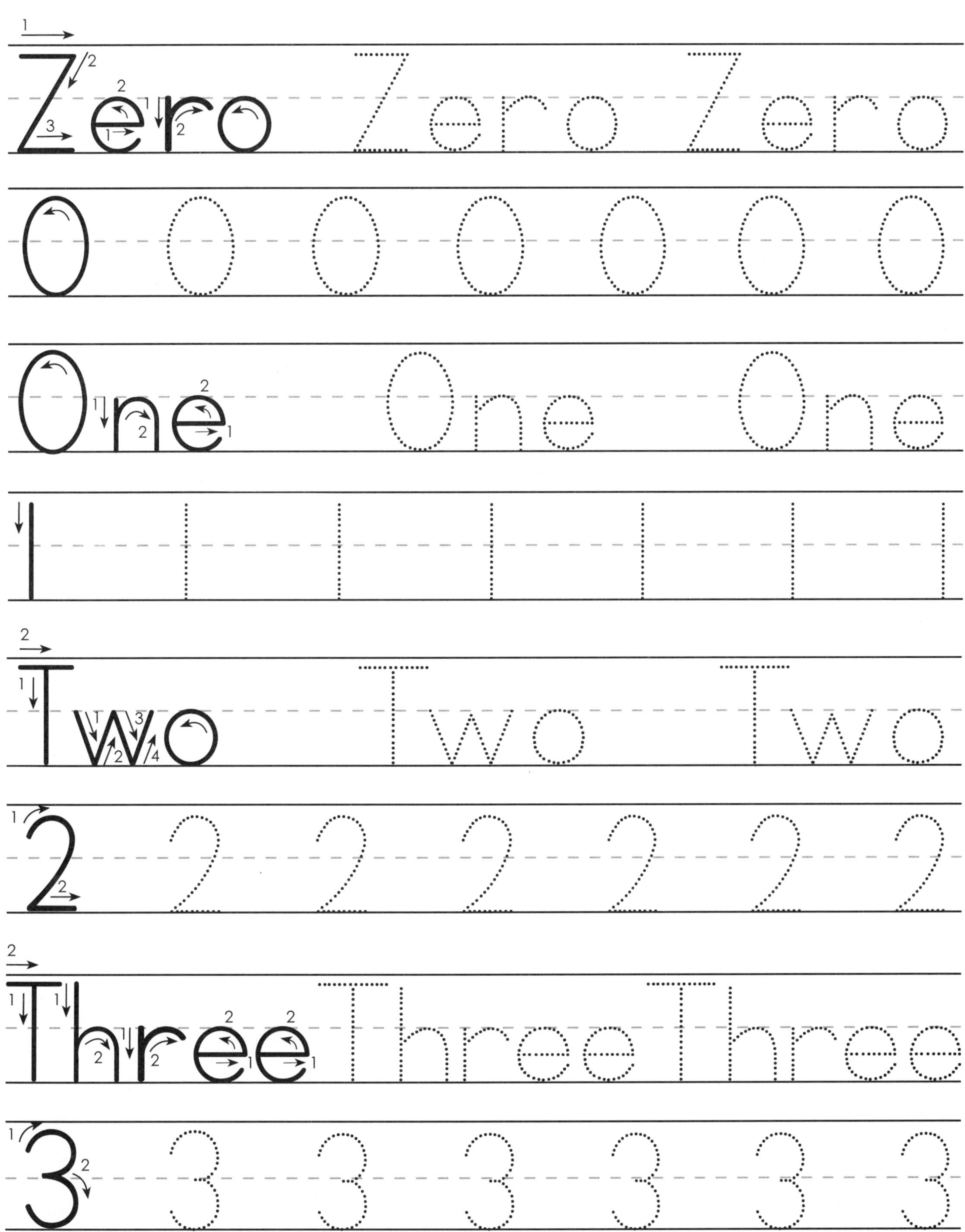

Colour and trace the words and numbers.

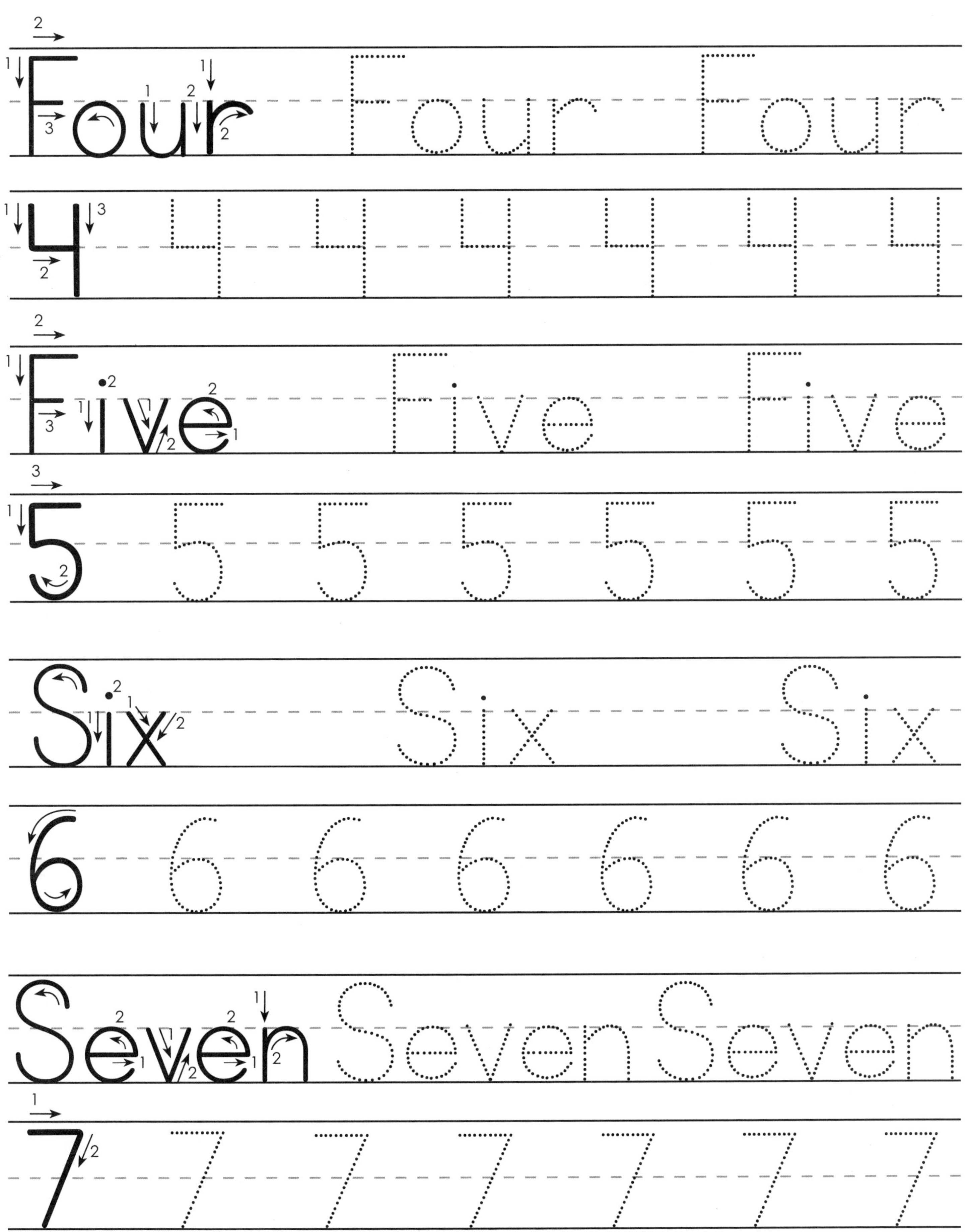

Colour and trace the words and numbers.

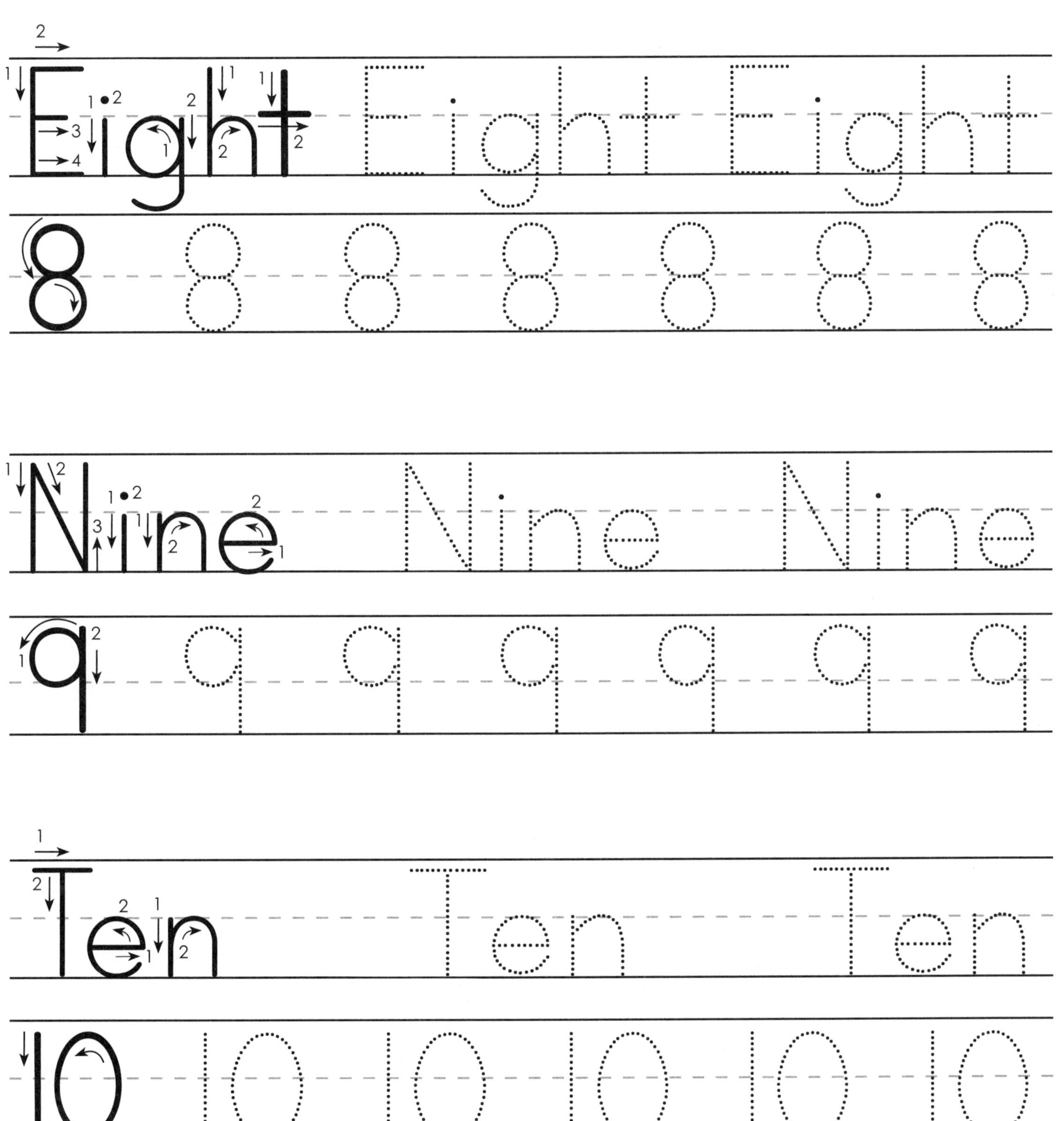

Trace the numbers.

Trace the words.

Now colour the pictures.

Trace the words.

Now colour the pictures.

Trace the words.

Seven

7 snakes 7 snakes

Eight

8 books 8 books

Nine

9 eggs 9 eggs

Now colour the pictures.

Trace the words.

Ten

10 farm animals

Now colour the pictures.